Ernst Billgren

What is Art
and 100 other very important questions

Translated by Carl Fredrik Gildea,
Eva Tofvesson Redz, Amesto Translations

Bokförlaget
Langenskiöld

The most common approach to writing about art is to describe what you think about it. Opinions are like feelers that we plunge into the boiling broth of culture where we find our bearings. Is this really the best approach? The world of art lacks a Linnaeus, someone who at some point catalogued and sorted everything out. Facts, not opinions. If Linnaeus had written down what he personally thought of all the plants instead (bluebell = beautiful, cactus = ugly), botany would not have become the science it is today.

In this book, I stay clear of opinions and attempt to remain true to the facts – facts which you should not take at face value, but rather verify with simple experiments. If I should still be in error in any of my answers, I gratefully look forward to receiving the correct one as soon as possible. Send it to: art@ernstbillgren.com. I promise to give you a reward.

The reader may discover that some of my answers appear contradictory. Does that imply that one of them is wrong? Not necessarily, since paradoxes are something you have to put into the equation, especially if you work with art or physics. For instance, it has been shown that elementary particles display unusual and paradoxical traits: they can be in several places at once – which is something many artists have to resort to as well.

1. Will knowledge resolve my artistic problems?
2. Should you do something good?
3. If you were to give a single piece of advice to a budding artist, what would it be?
4. What is art?
5. Isn't there a danger that you will stagnate over the years?
6. Is it not enough to do what you want?
7. How important is it that you create something new?
8. Does rebellion serve a function?
9. Why do so many people have a hard time understanding art?
10. What kind of teachers should you find for yourself?
11. Is it important to provoke?
12. What is the best way to exhibit your art?
13. Should you be self-critical?
14. How do you avoid making mistakes?
15. Is it important to promote your work?
16. How do you become independent?
17. Why does everybody have an opinion about art?
18. What should you begin with?
19. What should you keep in mind when choosing a gallery?
20. Which political outlook should an artist have?
21. Is it important to experiment?

22. Is it true that you only gain recognition when you are dead?
23. How do I become successful?
24. I have some "shortcomings" as an artist that I cannot cope with. What is the best way to work my way through them?
25. I am criticized for being unclear. Should I become more exact?
26. How do you learn things?
27. What is the purpose of art?
28. Why do people see such different things in a picture?
29. Should you specialize early on?
30. Should you question everything?
31. How do you make up something?
32. Is criticism good?
33. Why do we find some things beautiful?
34. Should you break conventions?
35. What makes you a good artist?
36. How do you know that you are on the right track?
37. Should I paint abstractly or figuratively?
38. Why such a fuss about artists that has nothing to do with their art?
39. What should you concentrate on?
40. I am torn between two different work methods, which one should I choose?
41. Were not artists more knowledgeable in the old days?

42. How do you speak intelligibly about art at a party?
43. How do you arrive at the center of art?
44. How do you become a content and happy artist?
45. My brother thinks my paintings are ugly. Could he be right?
46. Where have all the artists that were popular twenty-five years ago gone?
47. If you were to give a single piece of advice to a budding artist, what would it be?
48. Should society support "normal" or alternative art?
49. Why does everything feel empty and meaningless sometimes?
50. Is it important to succeed?
51. Should you work rapidly or slowly?
52. Why should you exhibit?
53. Who decides whether art is good or not?
54. Why do some artists keep repeating themselves?
55. Why does the concept of quality exist in art at all?
56. I am 39 years old. Am I too old to start painting?
57. How should you treat colleagues?
58. If you see an ugly work of art at an exhibition, should you comment on it?
59. How do I get people to appreciate my work?

60. How do I discover my conventions about art?
61. Why can I not stand certain artists and certain kinds of art?
62. Everything seems to have been done already, what is there left for me?
63. Why is art so difficult?
64. Can you not become too self-confident?
65. What is art?
66. How do you succeed abroad?
67. What should you think about when you are painting?
68. I have too little energy, how do I find more?
69. What are the chances that I will do something sensible?
70. I question myself when my teachers nag at me. How do I avoid criticism?
71. What is the difference between choosing and creating?
72. How come people steal my ideas so quickly?
73. What will be the next "new" breakthrough in art?
74. When you ask for advice you always get different answers. Who should you believe?
75. Must you understand what you are doing?
76. What will tomorrow's artist look like?
77. I have two different strands in my painting. Should I try to become more consistent?
78. Sometimes I like things that I later learn are bad. Am I wrong?

79. Should you try to avoid being arrogant and smug as an artist?
80. Why do people on other continents have such poor taste?
81. Which direction should your studio window face?
82. Does the value of my work matter?
83. What is taste? Why do we like some things and not others?
84. What should you say in an interview?
85. Should you appear in the media?
86. Why do so many artists paint old-fashioned and ugly?
87. What should you forget?
(Question posed by Swedish artist Dan Wolgers)
88. Why do people have such idiotic opinions about everything?
89. Is it important to be capable at your craft?
90. Is it possible to be both a contemporary artist and a painter?
91. What should you avoid?
92. What do I need to learn in order to be a good artist?
93. Why do so many, who have gone to art school, quit later?
94. How can you learn the most and better than others?
95. Is it important to earn money from your art?

96. Is it important to have a message?
97. My parents are artists, what is more important, nature or nurture?
98. How do you make art for eternity?
99. Do female artists not have the same value as male artists?
100. Where is the best place to exhibit your art?
101. Should and may I steal from others?
102. People think that my works are too blurred, should I become more distinct?
103. How do you know that you have the right opinion?
104. How do I know if I am working with the right things?
105. Why am I disappointed?
106. How do I paint as similar as possible?
107. What should you learn during your schooling?
108. How do you know if a painting is good?
109. Are there any good books if you are learning to make art?
110. Why are you so interested in foxes? (The most common question I get.)
111. Does megalomania help?
112. Is it important to have good taste?
113. Why is there so much written about peculiar art?
114. Why do people have such differing opinions about art?

115. How much of what you read in
 the newspapers about art can you trust?
116. Can you claim that if you know the most,
 you will be best?
117. What is art?

1.
Will knowledge resolve my artistic problems?

Short answer:

Only if you can make use of it.

Long answer:

791 persons were killed by toasters in the U.S. last year, but during the same period only nine persons were killed by sharks. Now, that is useful knowledge. Unfortunately, this information has not made people more afraid of toasters than of sharks, even if they ought to be. It is probably only at the moment we are roasting to death because of a crummy toaster that we remember: "That's right! Toasters are dangerous." Many people prefer to die rather than replace their delusions with facts.

2.
Should you do something good?

Short answer:

Not necessarily.

Long answer:

The stress and pressure to do something well is very high and somewhat impressive. It makes you lose focus on what you are actually interested in and will always guide you toward the accepted and general ideas that dominate the agenda of the day. Better, then, to do something and attempt to enjoy the result (as many do with their children) than to attempt to remake what you have done into something good (as many people do with their children). Art that history has deemed important is often a reflection of the prevailing *Zeitgeist*. Had the artist tried to accomplish something good instead of something true, it would have become less important; the desire to accomplish something good can be seen as a form of self-censure.

3.

If you were to give a single piece of advice to a budding artist, what would it be?

Short answer:
Paint the sky first, then the trees, so that you won't have to mess around with the sky between the branches.

Long answer:
This answer does not necessarily apply only to painting – the logic is applicable to all artistic pursuits. If you want to attain something, you should see your work as a logical and practical process. Many artists never achieve the results they aspire to, getting stuck in meaningless physical problems. Hence such ludicrous slogans as "the road itself is the goal" etc. That is the voice of those who never walked the entire length of the road and therefore never arrived at the goal.

4.
What is art?

Short answer:

A question.

Long answer:

Just as a physicist is a collection of atoms trying to discern what an atom is, so art is an invention that aims to discover what art is.

5.

Isn't there a danger that you will stagnate over the years?

Short answer:

You are joking, aren't you?

Long answer:

Nobody has ever discovered anything of importance after the age of thirty. Take Einstein for example: he made all his discoveries in youth and spent the rest of his life exploring his "Theory about Everything" (Grand Unified Theory – gut), which he never completed. You become more experienced over the years and can further develop your ideas, but your discoveries come at an early age. That is why many important works are "created" by aging artists – refined versions of their youth's somewhat clumsy discoveries. This should be accepted with humility. Both roles are equally important, but in different eras, one or the other has been considered more hip. Avoid pretending that you belong to "the wrong group" and act the youthful discoverer all your life – or the other way around.

6.
Is it not enough to do what you want?

Short answer:

Who knows what he wants?

Long answer:

For many people, the gap is too great between what they believe they want and what they really want. Their ideals disorient them. Many of them want to disregard what other people think, but in reality they are very interested indeed in other people's opinions and are disappointed when no one comes to witness their accomplishments. Or perhaps their ideals encourage them to work with the environment or with social issues, when they are actually more interested in, say, shoes or rodents. Or the other way round. And when the discrepancy between what they do and who they really are becomes too wide, indifference moves in, and while everything seems to be going great, suddenly nothing feels urgent anymore.

7.

How important is it that you create something new

Short answer:

Completely decisive.

Long answer:

Originality is the artistic quality that has been most strongly prioritized throughout the whole epoch of Modernism. There are no works of art in any of our modern art museums that is considered important that are not also innovative in some respect. However, throughout history this is a quality that has been largely dismissed. The Egyptians, for instance, did not care much for such matters, which is why it is difficult to discern the work of one generation from the next. The art was very good anyway, so it was not dependent on being original. It is not impossible that in the future, when Modernism has waned, we will accomplish great works that contain nothing new. However, we are not there yet.

8.
Does rebellion serve a function?

Short answer:

Yes – it is builds your self-confidence.

Long answer:

A revolt against something means you know something that others do not, that you have seen through the lies, understood that things are bad and often see how things ought to be instead. This is a wonderful emotion. When I studied at Valand Art College, I put up a sign in my studio that read "Refuse to rebel", since regardless of whether you rebel or conform you are dependent on the established order – both the rebel and the yes-man are un-free. Thus the danger with revolting is that you sacrifice your independence for a bit of self-confidence.

9.
Why do so many people have a hard time understanding art?

Short answer:

Because there is seldom anything there to understand.

Long answer:

Many people confuse understanding with liking: they remark that they do not understand something when they actually mean that they do not like it. However, ever since Modernism, artists have taken an interest in finding new "languages" in art; try entering a room with people who have invented new languages and I promise that you will be utterly bewildered. Just because you possess a new language does not necessarily mean that you have something to say. Only a few hundred years ago, the language of art was a common parlance and everyone could understand the images painted on a church wall – the message was more important than inventing a new language. As the pace of development accelerates, more energy is wasted making up new languages. You cannot understand someone who has not said anything, but you can like him.

10.
What kind of teachers should you find for yourself?

Short answer:
Bad ones.

Long answer:
Picasso, Matisse and many of the great artists had lousy teachers and they saw through them at an early stage, thereby quickly succeeding to establish their own artistic path. I have colleagues who have had excellent instructors, and with few exceptions they now work as instructors themselves, because that is what an excellent instructor teaches: how to perform as an excellent instructor! You can learn a few things from a poor instructor, then you can condone him/her and carry on your own. You come to the realization that there is no help to be had.

11.
Is it important to provoke?

Short answer:

Refrain from provocation – that normally infuriates people.

Long answer:

Many people in the art world say that they appreciate provocation, which in itself is an anachronism, or just a sign that what was meant to provoke has failed to do so. The idea with provocation should be to infuriate people, to irritate them, drive them up the wall. When people say they appreciate provocation in essence what they mean is that they enjoy that others feel provoked. To really provoke someone is easy: just scratch his car with a key. An artistic provocation is much more difficult, especially if the provocation is directed towards an audience of art connoisseurs. That is why provocation normally only works on people who are genuinely uninterested in art.

12.
What is the best way to exhibit your art?

Short answer:

All ways are good and bad.

Long answer:

There are three main venues to choose between:

1. Via curators: Get discovered by someone knowledgeable, who will arrange exhibitions at art halls and museums. Good option: you can create non-commercial art, enormous installations that take up a lot of space, videos and so on, but the risk is that your curator will soon grow tired and want to show something new by somebody else; you will lack your own platform.

2. A gallery: Exhibit and sell your work at a gallery. You risk becoming dependent on the forces of the art market, and you will find it difficult to work with, for instance, meat or other inconvenient materials. However, if you fit in, it can go really well and you might be exhibited in a chain of galleries. If the gallery owner grows tired of you, the assembled worth of your work will protect you from disappearing and you will easily find a new art gallery owner.

3. The Göransson Method: Åke G. rolled up all his stuff, put it in his mother's old sofa-bed and there it remained until someone discovered it. The drawback with this method is that it may take a while to achieve success, but this method has a high mythological potential, just look at van Gogh, for whom it worked splendidly.

13.
Should you be self-critical?

Short answer:

No.

Long answer:

Self-criticism, in the sense "I am stupid, bad, and so on" is merely self-destructive, whereas self-analysis and questions such as "What happened? Did the work turn out the way I wanted? Why did I want this? What would happen if?" can be very constructive. Self-criticism is an arresting force; if you ride your bike and think of all the things that you do when you rida your bike (steer, pedal, balance, etc.) you will most likely end up in a ditch soon. But if you get your speed up, you can even let go of the handlebars without losing control. Looking back at what you have created, you may realize that more often than not, you saved the disappointing works and discarded the promising ones. This will happen again, since you always imagine that you can determine what is good at the present moment. You are always capable of performing much better than what your taste tells you. Self-criticism is a drug to be ingested in tiny, well-diluted doses. Better, then, to realize that you do not have a clue to what is going on and release the hopefully small qualities you may be in possession of; if you lack any desirable qualities, what does it really matter if you are self-critical or not?

14.
How do you avoid making mistakes?

Short answer:

Do not avoid them – that would be a mistake!

Long answer:

Many psychological counselors in sports world work hard to teach their adepts not to avoid mistakes, since this cripples their performance abilities. A famous skater won silver medals at the Olympic and World Championships, and after consulting a psychologist they came to the conclusion that he was scared of falling in the turns. In the next competitions, he kept falling in the turns, only to win all the gold medals the following year. He had been wasting one percent of his energy and concentration on not falling in the turns and that was enough to keep him finishing as the runner-up. On the other hand, what's wrong with being a runner-up?

15.
Is it important to promote your work?

Short answer:
No, but it's lots of fun!

Long answer:
The wheel as an invention and the discovery of fire didn't exactly catch onon account of global marketing campaigns. Rather, it was the nature of their functionality that made them indispensable and popular inventions. Do something worthwhile and word will get out, with or without promotion. Still, marketing and the media can be enjoyable materials to work with, often with grand reactions as a consequence of your work, which can produce further platforms to explore. However, then the "promotion" becomes an end in itself.

16.
How do you become independent?

Short answer:

Never trust anybody.

Long answer:

Pretty soon you realize that you cannot rely on others' opinions and judgment, since all that is formed by their own circumstances and conventions. Even worse when you realize that you cannot rely on yourself, because you too are formed by your circumstances and conventions, as human beings are creatures of habit. What can you rely upon? A modest proposal would be to begin with a notion or a passing whim and let this fancy determine your work, at least that way you avoid remaining bound by your pre-conceptions. Another possibility is to bang yourself in the head with a hammer, as figures like Hill and Josephson, whatever else may be said of these guys, they do display a formidable degree of independence.

17.
Why does everyone have an opinion about art?

Short answer:

Truly incomprehensible.

Long answer:

Art, of all things, is a subject that everyone deems they are experts on, even though the training to become an artist is on average the same length as to become a brain surgeon. Still, most people would never dream of passing judgment on or proffering advice to a surgeon about to operate on a patient, and were they to do so, the surgeon would be somewhat taken aback. But when it comes to art, most people feel obliged to give their opinion or offer advice, no matter how ignorant they may be.

18.
What should you begin with?

Short answer:

Skip step one, two and three.

Long answer:

There are plenty of notions of what you must first master before you can even consider working as an artist: chromatics, *croquis*, and so on. Most often aspiring artists are put to work studying various crafts that must be learned first, probably with the intention of keeping away the competition. Skip the first steps and begin with the masterpieces. While working with a masterpiece, you will discover if you need to learn a particular skill or have to study some specific technique to finish your work. Learn what you need to know instead of struggling with an array of crafts that you may not need.

19.
What should you keep in mind when choosing a gallery?

Short answer:

How grand a frog you aspire to be.

Long answer:

If you manufacture parts for Volvo, you become dependent on Volvo, so try to master the whole chain of functions (production – the audience – the media – a gallery) in order to achieve maximum independence. Thus, starting out, it is perhaps wiser to find a small gallery with few good artists, than a more renowned and well-reputed one with a lot of good artists – all according to the principle: rather a grand frog at a smaller gallery, where you can influence things your way, than a petty frog at a top gallery, where you may not receive the attention you need and deserve.

20.
Which political outlook should an artist have?

Short answer:

A simple one, why not an extremist one?

Long answer:

A simple, non-contradictory *Weltanschauung* with simple solutions to all problems is convenient. It often fortifies you, not having to waste energy on doubts and weighing pros and cons or having to compromise. Consider the Leftists of the 1960's – few in number, but completely dominant in the fields of music, art and theater. Still, they produced a lot of good works within a short time span. Only when you are 100 percent certain that you are right can you commitall your energy to your words and actions, no matter how silly your opinions may be.

21.
Is it important to experiment?

Short answer:

Yes, but only before opening for business.

Long answer:

A chef, for instance, may play around and experiment with new combinations of ingredients. But if the restaurant only serves "Today's Experiment", it will soon be out of business, since the point of experimenting should be to arrive at something that can become a classic. No one should experiment for the purpose of arriving at an experiment. I have no objection to experiments, but when they become a household convention it is time to beware. Apart from the fact that they are seldom delectable, they have also lost their forward-moving, progressive function.

22.

Is it true that you only gain recognition when you are dead?

Short answer:

No.

Long answer:

99.99 percent of all artists gain notoriety while they are still alive. By the time they are dead, most of them are forgotten. There are some notable exceptions to this rule, such as Cézanne, van Gogh and a few others. These are parenthetical occurrences and probably won't occur again for ten thousand years. So, death is not your best bet.

23.
How do I become successful?

Short answer:

Make someone happy.

Long answer:

You become successful to the extent that someone else "profits" from your work, gets their ideals or notions validated, ideologically, economically, aesthetically or in some other way. This applies if you mean becoming successful in the eyes of others. If you mean successful in your own eyes, a touch of megalomania will do.

24.

I have some "shortcomings" as an artist that I cannot cope with. What is the best way to work my way through them?

Short answer:

Ignore them.

Long answer:

The more you work with a problem, the more of your attention and energy you put into it, and the problem is only amplified. Find out what lies behind the problem instead. The German general Heinz Guderian, who was the architect behind the concept of the *Blitzkrieg*, observed that the military command during World War I sent troops to the sites where opposition was fiercest, leading to an endless war in the trenches. So Guderian sent his troops to the areas where the resistance was weakest. The problem was thereby circumvented and dissolved as it no longer served a purpose.

25.

I am criticized for being unclear. Should I become more exact?

Short answer:
You are probably already right on target. Perhaps the question should be vaguer.

Long answer:
It is advisable to deliver approximate answers to all questions. When quantum physicists received different answers to the same question, lots of anomalies and outright errors in answer to the question what atoms consist of, they decided that the answer must be elastic – thus inventing the strings. In school you would have gotten the answer wrong if you claimed that four plus four equals something between five and twelve. But in quantum physics and in art that can be the exact answer.

26.
How do you learn things?

Short answer:

By misunderstanding.

Long answer:

You repeat and you mimic, and after a while you misunderstand something and the new notion is mimicked and repeated until you misinterpret yourself – and suddenly you have learnt something new. Knowledge is the convention of the hour and to avoid getting entrenched too early on, you should avoid conventions, for instance the one telling you to avoid conventions.

27.
What is the purpose of art?

Short answer:

If someone starts talking about the purpose of art, that person is probably a Nazi or something. Beware!

Long answer:

Totalitarian personalities and regimes have always hijacked culture for their own purposes and given it assignments that have seldom been conducive to art itself. Consider, for instance, social realism, which although it deserves some points for bungling, was destructive as a whole. A baker's task is to bake bread and an artist's task is to make art. If you want, you can try to save the world too, but that can never automatically become the task of all bakers simply because you think it is a sensible idea.

28.
Why do people see such different things in a picture?

Short answer:

You view things with your brain.

Long answer:

Everything we perceive is conditioned by learning. When we are born we see things upside down. Later we learn to turn the informational input around and it becomes more practical to see the ground below us. One scientist used eyeglasses with mirrors that turned everything he "saw" upside down. After a few months his brain turned the images right again so when he stopped using the glasses, everything was upside down. Transforming our three-dimensional world into a conceivable image in our head is always a fantasy, but we learn to use more or less common symbols for that which we perceive. Ask ten people which shade of green is greenest, and you will get ten different answers. Later, when you try to explain what you have perceived, further distortion follows, since language is also a subjective instrument. So, we still cannot compare what we think we may have seen.

29.
Should you specialize early on?

Short answer:

No need to, it comes with time, like sclerosis.

Long answer:

Many people attempt to start by specializing. After a few years they try to diversify their perspective – and then they give up. As for myself, first I dug the Sex Pistols, but after a few years I only liked their hit *God Save the Queen*. Some time later, I became completely spellbound by the short pause in the second verse and when I listen to that favorite section, the rest is silence.

30.
Should you question everything?

Short answer:

No.

Long answer:

It is important to know when to call into question and when to listen and obey. Most opinions and propositions are easy to contradict with the help of a little logic, since the opposite often is just as plausible and logical. The weight of an argument is dependent of whether you agree with it or not. Therefore you are best served by finding out what charges you with more artistic energy – agreeing or questioning.

31.
How do you make up something?

Short answer:

You create some space.

Long answer:

Making something up is about creating something from nothing. You create a space where things you never expected can "land", often through knowledge mixed with mistakes and other misconceptions. For example: Charles Goodyear was a shady figure who tried to palm off his rubber mail bags to the American Postal Service. The bags got sticky and ruined the mail and were just laying around in his workshop until one of them caught fire by mistake. That's how he discovered the method of vulcanization and today Goodyear is a major corporation. Accordingly, you should not be too meticulous in your work and dismiss all the irrelevant stuff, it might be of greater use to you than you might imagine. Everything irrelevant: anticipations, accidents and delusions create those excellent patches of space for ideas to land on.

32.
Is criticism good?

Short answer:

Yes, if it is productive. Not if it is contra-productive.

Long answer:

Criticism, at an art school for instance, is often constructive since it aims to improve the student's results. Criticism in newspapers is more diverse. It may be intended to help, but is often polemical, postulating the writer's opinion to be the right one, and so on. The purpose of the criticism is often transparent.The problem with criticism is that it always emanates from what you already know and is therefore automatically conservative – you cannot have a sensible opinion about things you are unfamiliar with. Criticism at its worst is when it tries to explain what the artist is doing and reveals the magic; critics are anti-cryptic by nature. Two wrong decisions can in the world of art lead to something good whereas excellent decisions may lead to something boring. Thus you may not be helped by proper guidance.

33.

Why do we find some things beautiful?

Short answer:

Because they are normal.

Long answer:

In one experiment photos were taken of ten people and from these a cross-image of the ten was digitally composed. The eleven photos were shown to people who were asked which one was most beautiful. Almost without exception was the eleventh picture chosen. We are probably programmed to appreciate the normal for reasons of reproduction.

34.

Should you break conventions?

Short answer:

Yes, rebels are always popular.

Long answer:

When you are young, you want to reveal the prevalent conventions and create a world view of your own, which can be repeated and transformed into a new convention that the next generation can break. When you are young you will do anything, as long as it is not boring, when you are old you will do anything, as long as it is not uncomfortable. The most important thing is to break those conventions that other do not break. Why not find some small meaningless convention that you will be the only one to break?

35.

What makes you a good artist?

Short answer:

Luck.

Long answer:

This may sound boring, since luck cannot be influenced? Sure it can. Here's an example: in a lottery, you can buy a whole pile of tickets and increase your chances of winning. Many believe that talent makes a difference, but it was difficult, for instance for a woman on Greenland five hundred years ago, to achieve a distinct artistic career. I do not know any, but it seems strange to believe that those women were less talented than other groups from other eras. Still, what's the point of being a good artist? Do not turn art into a competition.

36.

How do you know that you are on the right track?

Short answer:

By getting lost.

Long answer:

The advantage of not knowing where you are going is that you can never go in the wrong direction. It is only when you have decided on your goal that you can get lost. The problem is not that people get lost, but that they derive their ideas from their previous knowledge. A man was standing under a streetlight looking for the key he had lost. A passer-by helped him look for the key, but after a while he asked the man where he had lost the key: "I lost it over there, in the park." "In the park? Then why are you looking for the key here?" "Because it is lighter over here."

37.
Should I paint abstractly or figuratively?

Short answer:

No difference.

Long answer:

You cannot paint one or the other – it depends on the associative power of the beholder. If you paint a white square on a black background, you may consider it abstract whereas someone else will think it is a sugar cube. Is it an abstract painting then, or not? Is not everything abstract, anyway? For instance: a tree represents nothing except a tree, just as a square does not represent anything else than a square.

38.

Why such a fuss about artists that has nothing to do with their art?

Short answer:

Everything has to do with the artist.

Long answer:

The myth about something or someone is also called the brand. If you are uncertain about your ability to judge the quality of a commodity, you rely on the brand name. How many blind tests have you not heard of, where the testers give the higher grade to the lesser brand, say Pepsi, but the customers choose to buy Coca-Cola – even though they prefer Pepsi. Some exquisite art remains unnoticed whereas loads of worthless crap is very visible. Our art experience is governed by our concept of the art. Sometimes it can pay off to work on the myth about your paintings rather than waste your energy actually painting them.

39.
What should you concentrate on?

Short answer:

Nothing.

Long answer:

The problem with concentrating on something is that everything else automatically vanishes. The brain is like a one-dimensional slide projector – it can only focus on one thing at a time. Consider a simple cube: it can be viewed from above or from below, but never from both of these perspectives at the same time. When you work with art, a number of things have to work at the same time. It is more like a state, or a condition, than concentration.

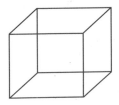

40.

I am torn between two different work methods, which one should I choose?

Short answer:

The third one.

Long answer:

If you are choosing between two things, the third solution is always the best one. Often you just get steamrolled by the third solution anyway while choosing between the first two. The problem is not choosing correctly but the choice itself. Creating is often an overwhelming experience, whereas insecurity, caution and deliberation are connected to choice. Your energy level becomes so low that both the alternatives you are choosing between become wrong. Creating is a much more productive path than choosing.

41.
Were not artists more knowledgeable in the old days?

Short answer:
Yep.

Long answer:
People are born more or less idiots, they understand nothing and know nothing, and when they die they are wise and filled with knowledge. Is this a mistake of nature? A waste of resources?

No. The problem is that it is harder to get rid of knowledge than to acquire it. All knowledge is a hindrance to development, just as dinosaurs hindered the evolution of primates. According to Ian Tattersall of the American Museum of Natural History, the alternative to extinction is stagnation. This does not mean that the small ugly mammals that survived the disaster were better than the smart, fast and strong raptors who met with their demise. If our dear old and wise artists had not died from natural causes, we would have to shoot them – not because they were wrong, since they then would be harmless, but because they were right.

42.

How do you speak intelligibly about art at a party?

Short answer:

You concur.

Long answer:

Now we are approaching the realm of the impossible. You must make the listener appear bright and if you want to say something you have to phrase it so that the listener feels as if he just thought it up himself. Elaborating on the benefits of Medieval scholasticism at a party is meaningless and most often appears silly, since most people in art, just like in sports, support a team regardless of whether it is good or bad. The best approach is to shut up. Ingrid Bergman did just that at one of the most charged moments in film history: she reset to zero since the scene itself defined her "expression". Had she resorted to acting the scene as well, it would have been tautological. Nobody wants to hear that they have the wrong opinion, especially not the ones who have the wrong opinion.

43.

How do you arrive at the center of art?

Short answer:
Not possible.

Long answer:
Starting out, you may feel like an outsider and want to get to the "center" of art. Like Dorothy in *The Wizard of Oz*, who after a long and adventurous journey finds the wizard at the center of the story, and pleads for help, only to discover that he is merely an old geezer with a megaphone but no power. The only thing she can do is take matters into her own hands and find her way home. It is a perfect analogy for how the art world works: there is no center and no help to be had. When you have walked the whole distance, you realize that you had been at the goal the whole time.

44.
How do you become a content and happy artist?

Short answer:

By having a goal greater than yourself.

Long answer:

Satisfying your ego is a tiresome and never-ending Sisyphean task. I have never encountered an artist who feels he is sufficiently well appreciated as an artist. Religious people often look happy when their actions serve a greater purpose than themselves – such as Mother Theresa, Dalai Lama among others, and people who have just saved the lives of lots of small children also tend to look pretty fulfiled. It's the same in art as with the rest of life: find a similar function in your art and you will end up happy and satisfied.

45.

My brother thinks my paintings are ugly. Could he be right?

Short answer:

Yes, everyone is always right.

Long answer:

If your brother likes yellow sports cars but hates red tractors, he is, of course, right, but this only says something about him, it doesn't says anything about either tractors or cars. The question you should ask yourself is whether it is important to you what your brother thinks. The answer is yes more often than you imagine, in which case you are faced with a choice: change brothers or change your art.

46.

Where have all the artists that were popular twenty-five years ago gone?

Short answer:

Working in their studios, as always.

Long answer:

Just because you do not notice them does not mean that they stop working, they only forgot to construct their own demise. Jesus is always a good guiding rule: he painstakingly participated in his demise only to be resurrected later. The other option is to fade away. Elvis Presley was pretty creepy in the 1970's, but is more popular than ever now. The more frequently you are denied (before the rooster crows), the greater the chance of being rediscovered. The public wants to appear interested, active, intelligent and non-conformist. Everybody knows how publicly decried Van Gogh and Picasso were, and the criticism stands in direct proportion to their popularity today. The question you have to ask yourself if you want to survive the 25-year-limit of attention is: How do I make myself as unpopular as possible?

47.

If you were to give a single piece of advice to a budding artist, what would it be?

Short answer:

Associate with those you want to be.

Long answer:

Humans are group creatures and are shaped by the group, as often demonstrated in candid camera episodes where people do all kinds of strange things just because others are doing them. Associate with lazy people and you will become lazy, and so on. It is not a coincidence that guys like Picasso and Matisse knew each other, teased each other, encouraged and spurned each other on. Find people whose energy you appreciate and stick to them.

48.

Should society support "normal" or alternative art?

Short answer:

Both.

Long answer:

Any alternative form of art is related to norms that it tries to distance itself from. Without norms, nothing is abnormal. The strength of the social fabric is derived from the wide range of qualities that co-exist. That is why there are fat people (endure starvation better), timid people (discover danger) and aggressive people (attack aggressors). A diversified group in the Stone Age cave contributed to the common survival of the tribe, whereas conformism would weaken the group. Good and bad art are dependent on each other like a net – much good art is created in relation to bad art, and vice versa. Take away bad art and good art collapses like a house of cards. Encourage all art.

49.

Why does everything feel empty and meaningless sometimes?

Short answer:

Congratulations.

Long answer:

You are in a splendid position. When you realize that everything is "meaningless", you can discover for yourself what you want to accomplish and why you want to accomplish anything at all, and pursue an independent artistic career. According to some psychologists, children today do not get bored enough, which cripples their creativity. Computer games, television and organized activities preclude the time they need to make up things by themselves. One day the sun will cease to exist, expand and burn up the Earth. Mountains will melt, the seas will evaporate and all life will finally cease to exist – a perspective good as any else to work from, when you are painting a still life with two melons and a vase, for instance.

50.
Is it important to succeed?

Short answer:

Yes!

Long answer:

Our brain functions on the basis of a punishment and reward system. Pain, for instance, signals that something is bad for us – like putting your hand in the fire – but can also exaggerate the danger – like agoraphobia. The brain rewards mating, eating, being well-rested, and so on, with feelings of satisfaction and happiness. Smoking, booze and sugar are ways to manipulate our reward systems, instilling treacherous feelings of pleasure. Better then to create a dependency on "succeeding" with your art, which is most probably also healthier for you than smoking. What it means to succeed with your art is up to you and anybody and not to be pontificated by others. Two thirds of those who attend art schools quit. That does not mean that they are worse artists than the one third who continue; rather they could not succeed in their own eyes. You cannot fool your reward system other than with chemicals.

51.
Should you work rapidly or slowly?

Short answer:

Neither.

Long answer:

The fewer ideals you have about how to work, the fewer inhibitions will paralyze you. Working slowly (Vermeer) is often considered more prestigious than working at a high pace (Picasso), but there are successful examples to be found in both categories. Working without such imposed ideals gives you the option of taking the amount of time your work of art requires.

52.
Why should you exhibit?

Short answer:

People who are under scrutiny sharpen their senses.

Long answer:

Many people avoid littering in the street if they know they are being observed, alcoholics who experience religious conversion fare better, since someone is always keeping an eye on them even when they are on their own. They shape up. If you know that your work will be exhibited it is harder to cheat. You examine yourself through other people's eyes. Another advantage with exhibiting is that you never really get to fully see your works in the studio – they become clouded by your own intentions, notions and ambitions. In an exhibition they become more exposed.

53.
Who decides whether art is good or not?

Short answer:

Glenn D. Lowry.

Long answer:

Quality is a moniker for what the people you respect appreciate. Even if you do not agree with them, there are those whom you perceive as authorities in the field on account of their expertise, their position or the respect they enjoy among their peers. Subsequently, what is considered geniality changes as those people are substituted. The Pre-Rafaelites were considered the best thing that had happened in the art world, but well into the twentieth century nobody defended them any longer and their work was automatically devalued as passé. The paintings themselves did not change over time. Quality is a relative term in a similar way as Time (which feels absolute in the present moment).

54.
Why do some artists keep repeating themselves?

Short answer:

Because they are not rats.

Long answer:

Studies have been conducted with rats, where they were placed in a maze with five boxes at the end. A piece of cheese was placed in the fourth box and the rat was put in the maze. After a while it found the piece of cheese in box four. The experiment was repeated and after only a few attempts the rat hurried directly to box four, where the cheese was waiting for him. Then they put the cheese in box two instead. The rat ran straight to box four but found no cheese, ran all the way back and checked the labyrinth, only to return to box four again; no cheese. After a while the rat began sniffing around and finally found the cheese in box two. The difference between rats and humans is that humans keep running back to box four the rest of their lives.

55.

Why does the concept of quality exist in art at all?

Short answer:

To avoid the bumps.

Long answer:

I have a similar function in my car. When you step on the gas pedal you accelerate moderately, and if you release the pressure, the speed decreases gently. Once, that function broke and the result was a very bumpy and inconvenient ride. Without any notion of quality, art would become too clumsy, unpredictable and incalculable to overview and appreciate. We possess the concept of quality because it is more convenient that way. An alternative to our concept of quality would be function, which is what was used for instance, in the Stone Age.

56.

I am 39 years old. Am I too old to start painting?

Short answer:

Probably.

Long answer:

Irrespective of age, it is almost impossible to become the kind of artist you feel comfortable being. Painting is something you do despite all the reasons against it. Van Gogh began late, never found a teacher because he was too bad, later that badness became a quality, but he never got the time to become "good". Many artists who were pretty lousy at drawing at school, never received the encouragement they needed, and nevertheless they accomplished something.

57.
How should you treat colleagues?

Short answer:

With friendliness, cheerfulness and gratitude.

Long answer:

It is easy to get the impression that the artist's job is a one-man enterprise, but if you were the only person on Earth, it is unlikely that your work would look the way it does, or even that you would have accomplished anything at all. Art is a group enterprise with an endless exchange of ideas, mixed with the ones that show you what it should not look like. Very useful. We are dwarfs on the shoulders of giants, and as such it behooves us to be cautiously friendly.

58.

If you see an ugly work of art at an exhibition, should you comment on it?

Short answer:

Never without being asked.

Long answer:

In the same way that you should not comment if someone has a big nose or ugly clothes – even if the person who asks is, e.g., your husband or wife. It always ends in a meaningless argument and it leads nowhere to point out the big nose as something unpleasant. People's art is no less a personal topic than their attire or facial features. However, if someone asks you and is really interested in your comment – go ahead. If you are invited to a dinner and the first thing you do is to remark that the hosts should have heated the plates, perhaps you will not be invited next time. Hence, the bad habit of commenting at exhibitions is unfathomable to me.

59.

How do I get people to appreciate my work?

Short answer:
Stop wondering.

Long answer:
People love people who do not worry or give a damn about what others think, who possess an independence based on a self-assumed task, letting this mission and not other people's opinions determine their artistic vision. Focus on your task and stop worrying: that is the fastest road to appreciation.

60.
How do I discover my conventions about art?

Short answer:

Write them down.

Long answer:

Write down what you feel important about art and without further ado you will have a list of the conventions and forced concepts that you are stuck with.

61.

Why can I not stand certain artists and certain kinds of art?

Short answer:

In order to remain sane.

Long answer:

Experiments – unusually cruel ones – have been conducted with rats, where a red lamp is lit and a few seconds later the rat is given an electric shock. After repeated exposure, the rat will go crazy when the red lamp is lit, and die. However, if you place a cage with another rat next to the shocked rat, then as soon as the red lamp is lit, the shocked rat will attempt to attack his neighbor. He will blame his discomfort on his neighbor and get to vent the frustration of his discomfort. This rat, now with an enemy, will thrive and survive much longer than a rat without an enemy. You need someone to blame or else you die. The alternative is to like everything and not find any art disquieting, which is more difficult.

62.

Everything seems to have been done already, what is there left for me?

Short answer:

Look a little bit to the side of what you are staring at.

Long answer:

Even if you walk a hundred miles along an endless road, you still have an endless stretch of road left to walk. When you discover or invent something, it often appears obvious and simple in hindsight. The present works like the blind spot in your eyes, it can only be discovered if you look a bit to the side of what you are regarding. Good inventions are sprung from actual needs, thus it is more interesting when you made the discovery than what you discovered.

63.
Why is art so difficult?

Short answer:

Difficult? Being an artist is the easiest job in the world.

Long answer:

It may be perceived as difficult since it is impossible to fail at. Play tennis and you can win or lose – play the game without rules, lines and net and it will not work. The same applies to art. In a world without lighthouses it can be difficult to navigate. That is why it can feel difficult, but you always hit something, although you may not be one hundred percent sure whether the ball was in or out.

64.
Can you not become too self-confident?

Short answer:

Sure, in your head, but not with your hands.

Long answer:

If you are certain about something it almost always means that you have not understood the whole problem. Reality is full of paradoxes and our brain is not equipped for this: it prefers either-or. Either something is short or long. Standing in front of an object that is both short and long we become confused and normally decide for one alternative, since it is so incredibly hard to identify something as both short and long. The problem is that you never are never done. The gap between what you planned and what you create must not become too great. If you are confident and have gathered experience in your hands, you will not need to use your head and deal with paradoxes.

65.
What is art?

Short answer:

A word.

Long answer:

The question "What is art?" is a linguistic problem, not an artistic one. All concepts have a beginning and an end. Consider the word "dead", that normally signifies "lifeless" and has in the past one hundred or so years developed to also mean "exactly" – a considerable change in meaning. Neanderthals did not enter caves and paint to create art, they did it to appease their gods and create good fortune for their hunting. The concept of art, the way we understand it today, seems to have appeared in the 18th century, and then, at the turn of the previous century, everyday utility goods (so-called ready-mades) became objets d'art. Since then more and more things and events have taken up residence in the concept of art. Nowadays any kind of happening or object can be art. A concept that does not exclude anything at all lacks function. Personally, I believe that the concept of art became defunct in the 1960's, but that we have not quite grown accustomed to this fact yet.

Art is a three hundred-year-old parenthesis. Had we instructed a coach driver long ago to take us "dead ahead", he may have driven us straight to a cemetery. That is where the concept of art belongs.

66.

How do you succeed abroad?

Short answer:
You live there.

Long answer:
At a certain time in their careers, many artists get a few opportunities to exhibit their work abroad, but later encounter difficulties following these up. The Japanese conquered most of Asia with a certain ease and Napoleon invaded Moscow. But in both cases, the supply lines were too long and they lost everything. An area is only conquered when it has been held for a while. Concentrate your activity on smaller areas, but be dominant in that field and grow slowly but steadily. Choose fields that you can defend – you or a representative must be present. Art is dialogue. You must have a someone to talk to. Who remembers who exhibited what at some bygone biennial?

67.

What should you think about when you are painting?

Short answer:

It doesn't matter.

Long answer:

What a cannonball thinks of, as it bursts through the air, does not affect where it will strike. What really matters is what you aim at, the size of your cannon and how much gunpowder you use to fire it. Any thinking should be done before the shot is fired.

68.

I have too little energy, how do I find more?

Short answer:

You have plenty, get started.

Long answer:

According to Einstein, the average human being contains energy equivalent to at least one hundred atomic bombs (7 times 10^{18} Joule). There is no lack of energy, only some trouble releasing it. In an atomic bomb explosion about one percent of the energy contained in the uranium is released. In other words, there is no lack of energy, only a lack of self-discipline. Get started, conceive something and then just do it. The energy is there, but maybe not the passion? In that case, switch to something that interests you. The easiest things to do are ones that are a matter of life and death.

69.

What are the chances that I will do something sensible?

Short answer:

The same.

Long answer:

Something remarkable happened the other day. I saw a man with a beard in a red top cap chewing gum and buying tomatoes and mustard at a local mini-market. As long as I live, this sight will probably never be repeated. The odds that this would happen again is one in a billion of billions. But when it happens, it is one hundred percent true that it is happening and looks so utterly normal - so normal that you will hardly even notice it. Life itself is a sequence of almost impossible events, just as impossible as if you were to do something sensible.

70.

I question myself when my teachers nag at me. How do I avoid criticism?

Short answer:
Duck.

Long answer:
It is important to continue with the task you have set for yourself, even after facing criticism. Many important works have begun as failures, but the artist persevered and never gave up. That is why it is especially important to continue with your idea, even if the criticism is justified. It is a bloodbath out there, so entrench yourself and create some "dummies" for them to aim at. During World War II they invented inflatable tanks that the enemy was tricked into wasting their ammunition on. Paint something very ugly and show that to your teachers. Keep what is important to yourself.

71.

What is the difference between choosing and creating?

Short answer:

They are exact opposites.

Long answer:

Making a choice is a passive action, while creating is a radical one. You always make your choices based on knowledge, for instance which newspaper you prefer. Choosing is a very conservative activity. I myself, no matter how carefully I deliberate, almost always order the same kind of pizza. One vacation, as an experiment, I chose everything differently: different postcards, different food, different souvenirs. It resulted in more or less the same quality of life. What we choose seldom makes a great difference. When a chaffinch perceives imminent danger from several directions (dog at the right, cat at the left, falling piano from above), it proceeds to preen itself, as a form of mental defense. Our equivalent of the finch's preening is choosing – instead of doing what we should be doing. Creating something is an eye-opening experience. Many artistic careers consist 99 percent of making choices, for instance, which color to use – thus little is created. Increase the amount of creating and minimize the choosing.

72.
How come people steal my ideas so quickly?

Short answer:

Figure that one out and you deserve an award.

Long answer:

There are monkeys on the Japanese islands that eat potatoes. In the beginning, they only ate the clean bits, until one monkey dropped his potato in the water, probably by accident, and subsequently could eat the whole potato. All monkeys on that island followed suit and began washing their potatoes, no big surprise, but shortly after this, monkeys on the neighboring islands also began to wash their potatoes, although no contact existed between the islands, and monkeys can´t swim. There is an award offered to whoever can explain how this happened. Many shoals of fish turn simultaneously. Already in 1925, Wolfgang Pauls discovered that certain subatomic particles know what other subatomic particles are doing, even when separated by enormous distances, which has been confirmed in laboratories during the 1990's. They do not steal your ideas, you are just all washing your potatoes at the same time.

73.

What will be the next "new" breakthrough in art?

Short answer:

The absence of Modernism.

Long answer:

Plurkevass! Nobody can understand this word, because it is a word and a language that I just made up. Modernism is crammed with new languages. Hence the distance between art and its audience which did not exist earlier, for instance in the Middle Ages, when everyone knew that if you did not behave, you would burn at the stake. First, new languages (cubism, surrealism, etc.) emerged because so many new phenomena arose that the old languages were not suited to describe. After a while, new languages continued to be invented out of pure habit, even if there was nothing new to be said. Once the urge to create new languages has subsided modernism can finally come to an end and the possibility to create something completely new will unfold.

74.

When you ask for advice you always get different answers. Who should you believe?

Short answer:

All of them.

Long answer:

Art is full of lies and conjecture. Its present status is comparable to, say, medicine in the thirteenth century. Very few facts, and a whole lot of opinions and guesswork. In those days, walnuts were considered to be effective against headaches, because they look like a small brain. Nowadays, people prefer to take an aspirin. "The road is the goal" and "Less is more" are examples of typical Orwellian lies. Less is, of course, less, and more is more. Listen to everyone's answers, but check if they are accurate. Most of them can be checked with simple experiments. In school, a teacher once told us that you have to draw "with feeling". Instead of accepting her idea, I proceeded to draw one picture "with feeling" and one without "feeling", and asked people to identify which one was drawn with feeling. I even asked others to repeat my experiment. It turned out that no one could see the difference. If it is all that important, it does not seem to be something you can influence, and so it is meaningless to say or think so.

75.

Must you understand what you are doing?

Short answer:

Not necessarily.

Long answer:

Some successful artists work intuitively while others have a more intellectual approach. It's better to work with something that functions but that you do not understand than with something you understand but does not work. Sometimes your understanding distracts your focus from whether it is working or not. The beauty of understanding what you are doing is that it gives you the possibility to repeat and emphasize what is working well. By the time you start wondering whether you want to be an intellectual artist or a "naive" one, it is probably already too late.

76.
What will tomorrow's artist look like?

Short answer:

Blurred, like now but worse.

Long answer:

When I began with art, there was only one higher art school in Sweden, and when I graduated there were five. The number of artists has increased dramatically, whereas the number of exhibition venues remains constant or, according to some, has decreased. Put differently: a career through the galleries is not a viable option for most artists and there are not enough attics in Paris to make that a workplace option. How much stuff do we need when half the population chooses to become artists, and every kid wants to work within a creative line of business? In the future, artists will work in groups and cooperate, working on projects together with organizations and companies. Larger corporations will hire an artist as an inventive make-believer, but most work will be found in the area of popular culture. The artist's profession will blend with other roles and vanish as a category of its own. Since the new technologies enable everyone to make movies, music, start a television channel, and so on. Until recently, even painting in oil was only possible for a select few, since paint was not readily available in the stores. The artist as a specialized professional category did not even exist until the coming of industrialism. People moved to cities and went to work instead of living in the countryside, doing a little of this and that; in the information age it seems as if we will have more flexible professional boundaries, and so also the artists.

77.

I have two different strands in my painting. Should I try to become more consistent?

Short answer:

No, it is better with two good strands than one bad one.

Long answer:

At my book store, the most popular books are cookbooks, closely followed by books about horses. These two genres keep the book business afloat. They provide the profit that supports the publication of more demanding literature. If you would combine these two winning genres and publish a cookbook with horse recipes, it is not at all certain that this book will become an even greater success. One plus one does not always make two, and in the world of art, practically never.

78.

Sometimes I like things that I later learn are bad. Am I wrong?

Short answer:

Yes, congratulations!

Long answer:

The more you know, the less you like. You often specialize and fewer things appear interesting from that narrower perspective. A side effect is that the more things you dislike, the less interesting the rest of the world appears. A person who likes everything is living in paradise, a person who dislikes everything lives in hell. Accordingly, it is smart to like as much as possible, although this may be difficult.

79.

Should you try to avoid being arrogant and smug as an artist?

Short answer:

Too late.

Long answer:

There are two types of people – those who know that they are arrogant and those who do not know. Unfortunately, it is not so that it is the good people who create good art, while the wicked and smug ones mess around making bad art, which would have been fairer. People from both groups make both bad and good art. Rather, it is the need to express yourself and the energy that derives from your personality that are the deciding factors.

80.

Why do people on other continents have such poor taste?

Short answer:

They inherit it.

Long answer:

Taste, opinions and belief systems are normally not personal, but are inherited locally. It's a no brainer that most Yankee fans are born in New York and Lakers fans in Los Angeles. If everyone chose for themselves where they were to live, people of the same persuasion would not be so packed and extremely geographically locked together. Most Moslems live in Arabic countries, while most Hindus are born in India. Were people to decide for themselves there would probably be fifty percent living in either place. Furthermore, it is only human to feel that everything that your opponents think or believe is abhorrent to you. Just ask a Mets fan what he thinks about the Yankees.

81.
Which direction should your studio window face?

Short answer:

None.

Long answer:

The whole idea of skylight in studios dates from the Middle Ages when lighting was bad or nonexistent. The drawback with the sun is that it gives varying shades of light all the time, depending on the temperature or the angle. If you paint in sunlight and later hang the painting in a normal room, the colors will have changed completely. The painting should be created in the same light that it will hang in later. Use a light that is as neutral as possible if you are not sure where it will be exhibited. But if it is going to hang outdoors, it will do just fine to paint it in a studio with a skylight.

82.
Does the value of my work matter?

Short answer:

Not in the beginning.

Long answer:

Starting out, you are more attuned to the artistic values, but the economic value functions as a kind of protection. If Picasso's paintings had cost a mere twenty bucks a piece, they would be molding away in many an outdoor privy today. While instead they receive the best possible care at museums. On the other hand, a very high price can obscure the view of the work of art, and they become changed or even invisible behind the economic value. Everything in moderation. Still, value can serve as an indicator of quality. When did you ever see a cheap old painting hanging in a museum? And as a matter of fact, all ancient paintings that are considered masterpieces are expensive.

83.

What is taste? Why do we like some things and not others?

Short answer:

You like what you see.

Long answer:

That was Hannibal Lecter's reply in *Silence of the Lambs*. Liking something (desire), is a learning process, which became even more apparent to me when I began to drink green tea. It tasted horrible in the beginning. After a month or so, it didn't taste anything at all and now I cannot live without it. Consider the way people walk – changing your walking-style can feel unnatural, even if a lot of people would profit from improving the way they walk and thereby avoid back-pains. Personally, I believe that things around us possess certain qualities that we either like or dislike, whereas we, in reality, create our own experiences – the way we take in the world around us.

84.
What should you say in an interview?

Short answer:

It doesn't matter.

Long answer:

What people pick up from television and the papers varies enormously. I heard that the actress who played the part of the mother in *Home Alone* was beaten up by an angry woman at an airport, because "she was such a lousy mother". Keep in mind that television is an image-driven medium, so people might remember if you wore socks in different colors but maybe not what you said. You are never in just one TV program but in as many as there are viewers. If you absolutely must talk to the media, you should assume that no intellectual content will pass through the screen. Media is not the medium for transmitting ideas and thoughts, except possibly for this single message: this is what I look like at the moment and I am still alive.

85.
Should you appear in the media?

Short answer:

If you have the stamina!

Long answer:

Artists can work with all kinds of materials – traditionally this has been clay, colors, stone and so on. During the past century they have also worked with ready-mades, photography, installations, the audience, companies and, naturally, the media – a hard-worked material but with amusing qualities. People working in the media do not like people who appear in the media – instead they adore the ones who never grant interviews. This is probably some kind of self-contempt. Normal people think it is okay, but you should never care about what people think. They also love butter, sugar and cigarettes, but that does not necessarily mean that this is good for them. Media is a very wide but ephemeral material, as opposed to for instance bronze, which is narrower (smaller audience) but more durable. As with all materials, it is important to decide what you want to accomplish so that there are no unexpected surprises. Personally, people who keep popping up in the media all the time annoy me, and so does loud music in cafés. But I am still a cookie-lover, right?

86.

Why do so many artists paint old-fashioned and ugly?

Short answer:

Because they might as well.

Long answer:

A writer does not need new or nice-looking alphabetic letters to write an interesting text, he/she might as well use the same old ugly ABC. However, you do need new words for things you do not know. It's good to know on which level you should be creative and which junk is best to make use of.

87.

What should you forget?

question posed by Swedish artist Dan Wolgers

Short answer:

Should.

Long answer:

Your profession as an artist you must invent for yourself. Accordingly, all "musts" should be avoided. They can be difficult to discern, since without all musts you seem to gravitate freely in the universe. Try thinking about that the other way around instead, and more often the result is as good as your first inclination. I have heard that the universe is expanding and therefore all heavenly bodies are in flight away from each other. Couldn't it be so instead that all materia is shrinking and that is why it looks as if everything is on its way away from us? It sounds more logical, since most things tend to grow smaller with time, especially all "musts".

88.

Why do people have such idiotic opinions about everything?

Short answer:

They have no choice, which is lucky.

Long answer:

Opinions are automatic reactions to experiences and are never personal, but useful from an evolutionary perspective. If you get run over by a man with a red beard, you will probably nurture negative opinions about men with red beards. The wide range of opinions in a group of people is a strength and should be encouraged. Paradise is not a place where everyone shares the same opinions, rather it is a place where the neo-Nazi and the vegan sit barking at each other in a bar, only to walk homewards in the night, arm in arm, singing some song together. The place where everyone has the same opinion is hell. Consequently, it is never a good idea to shove your opinion down someone else's throat, even if you, of course, are right.

89.
Is it important to be capable at your craft?

Short answer:

Yes, but it is a dangerous place to hide.

Long answer:

It is, of course, splendid to do what you want to, or at least to know someone who can do it for you. But the danger of the craft is that it is easy to be fascinated by the craft, and get stuck in it. I met a sculptor who worked on a rolling-pin with bearings for two years, with wonderfully well-adapted wood and a perfect balance. This tool, used to roll out clay strings to moulds, technical rather that artistic solutions had won the upper hand in his life. Graphic and digital artists should be extra cautious in this respect, as these are art forms full of artisan skills and easy to be both inspired and engulfed by.

90.

Is it possible to be both a contemporary artist and a painter?

Short answer:

No, but it may be worth a try.

Long answer:

Torsten Andersson, a Swedish artist, discovered already in the 1960's that it was no longer possible to paint (except, possibly, monochromes). So he created paintings of sculptures instead, to circumvent the problem. I do not view my paintings as art, but as tools to create situations that amuse me and that may be art. The best approach is, as usual, to disregard the problem altogether.

91.

What should you avoid?

Short answer:

Nothing.

Long answer:

Avoiding something is a defensive approach. You often see how people who have invented or accomplished something good become too cautious and lose it all instead. Good soccer teams leading with 2 to 0 can begin to play so defensively that they lose the game. "What is the worst thing I can do right now?" is a reasonable motto to work by. Actively pursuing what you fear may come to be will guarantee that you avoid negative surprises.

92.

What do I need to learn in order to be a good artist?

Short answer:

Nothing.

Long answer:

Most people are filled with skills and continue to learn things for the rest of their lives out of pure habit, without using more than a few of their skills. Either because they do not know how to, since they have not trained how to use them, or they are not content with their skills and keep pursuing something they like. It is not so that skillful people create good art and the other way around. Surely that would have been fairer. Some have simply learned how to make use of and appreciate the great or small skills they possess.

93.

Why do
so many, who
have gone
to art school,
quit later?

Short answer:
Because they forget why they began in the first place.

Long answer:
Many people begin their schooling with great zeal and few skills, like a car with a big engine and a small steering-wheel. The more you learn, the greater the potential for you to steer your artistic career (larger steering-wheel) and the smaller the engine becomes. Finally, you have a giant steering-wheel and an engine that is completely run down. One problem is that the more you learn and the higher your ideals rise, the greater the wobbly play between who you are and what you do; that disadjustment creates tedium, and the car stops its progress.

94.

How can you learn the most and better than others?

Short answer:

By acting the idiot.

Long answer:

Waking up each morning with a "beginner's outlook" makes it possible for you to be receptive to new information. But if you already know everything, your chance to learn something new vanishes. Compare a full glass of water to an empty one. Which one can you pour new water into? Walking around acting dumb is thus the best approach, with the added bonus that others will appreciate you as nicer since they will perceive themselves as smart in comparison.

95.

Is it important to earn money from your art?

Short answer:

No, but it makes things easier.

Long answer:

Avoid mixing art with money in the same way as you should avoid mixing sex with money. Money may, however, be an important "color on your pallet" if you want to work with large or expensive projects or films. Gather as much as you can in the ways you know how so you can do as you please. Many artists throughout history have had a sales production with light-weight work that was easy to dispose of and spent the rest of their time working on their own stuff. Afterwards it often turned out that it was the stuff for sale that was their better work. The artist was perhaps not so high-strung when he manufactured them.

96.

Is it important to have a message?

Short answer:

Do not bother.

Long answer:

Today everybody has a message. We are drowning by newspapers, electoral cabins in the street and most of all by advertising, all the way into our homes through our mailboxes and in our computers. In an era when everybody has a message, it can be nice with art that shuts up. If you on the other hand have a message you absolutely want to spread, art may be an appropriate vehicle. But it is in no way necessary. Mona Lisa, for instance, manages pretty well without a message.

97.

My parents are artists, what is more important, nature or nurture?

Short answer:

It is the same thing.

Long answer:

Does it depend on nature or nurture that the giraffe has a long neck? Nature, of course, you may think, as his parents had long necks – but at the same time: if there had not been any trees higher than one meter, giraffes would not have had long necks at all, thus nurture. One cannot exist without the other – nature and nurture are practically the same thing. People from artistic homes often get an early start but can have a rougher time finding a voice of their own. On the other hand an artist should never care about whether he has the right preconditions or not.

98.
How do you make art for eternity?

Short answer:
Create life.

Long answer:
Eternity is probably too long a time-span, but say a few hundred thousand years. Everything breaks down: stone, metals, countries collapse, oceans move. The only thing with a chance to survive is life. Mosquitoes are still around, just like they were when dinosaurs walked the earth. Even dinosaurs are gone now, as are the landscapes that they lived in. If you transfer this to art it means that works and ideas that can create copies of themselves in turn will create copies and live on forever. One way to judge the charge of an idea is to appreciate the energy that you and others derive from it. Mountains get worn down, but energy is indestructible (but can be transformed). It is, thus, something positive when others steal your ideas and copy your work.

99.

Do female artists not have the same value as male artists?

Short answer:

Nope, they are completely worthless (just like male artists).

Long answer:

How much should they be worth? 230 million? Avoid searching your worth by comparing yourself to others or even to any standards outside yourself, and avoid everything that has to do with finding similarities. Look for dissimilarities and for everything that is unique about yourself. If something is worthless, it is also independent.

100.

Where is the best place to exhibit your art?

Short answer:
On Mars.

Long answer:
The context in which art is exhibited is more important than most people realize. There is no right or wrong, however there are very different results, and often the whole situation is more important than what you show. If someone on the first manned mission to Mars would happen to find a small painting under a stone portraying two small yellow triangles, this would stir an enormous attention and probably cause us to reevaluate the whole existence of the human race. Such a painting would probably be considered as one of the most important pictures in our history. If instead there were two green cubes in the painting, similar results would most likely be the case. If instead you exhibited any of these paintings at the local frame-maker, few passers-by would give a rats' ass.

101.

Should and may I steal from others?

Short answer:

Yes, but it is easier when you are young.

Long answer:

To young people, it seems natural to knick something. Look for instance at how almost every high school student googles instead of researching the subject of their essay or writing assignment, or the current formation of political parties in Europe with free downloading of music and film as their main vote-winners. They do so, as they do not feel as part of everything that already exists, and why – in these days and times – should they? Everything already existed to begin with, and it is difficult to both eat a cake and keep it. Their day of judgment will come when the next generation turns up and steals their stuff. Ignorance helps, as it is easier to discover things if you do not know that others have already invented them. If you are relatively unoriginal, irrespective of generation, you will pursue the ideals that are popular at the moment, for instance being unique. An independent artist on the contrary does exactly as he pleases and can therefore without embarrassment copy another artist. Only a free artist can indulge in being impersonal.

102.

People think that my works are too blurred, should I become more distinct?

Short answer:

To yourself: yes! To others: no!

Long answer:

A distinct and visible point with a work is like an anecdote with a punch-line, it's great the first time you hear it, doubtful the second time and worthless after that. If you want your work to last longer than that first glance, you should hide the "point" as well as you possibly can. The less distinct the point, the longer your work will last. The beholder will be the active one and can find his own "points" each time. However, it is good if you yourself have a precise notion about what your work aims at, as a propelling force during your creative process.

103.

How do you know that you have the right opinion?

Short answer:

Everybody has.

Long answer:

Most people are content with their opinions. I have never met anyone claiming that he has the wrong opinion, and if you are convinced by others, you can always change the opinions you started off with. The current view is that the Earth has always been round, even when everyone believed it was flat. But when people thought the Earth was flat, then they also believed that it would remain that way forever. Avoid opinions, they tie you down. Many people have opinions about everything and do as little as possible. Most opinions are out there already and do not need another adherent. Having an opinion makes you less curious. Opinions and prejudices are closely related. Opinions are like the *Matrix*, the "web" in the film with the same name – real reality lies beyond it. If people were aware of the fabric from which opinions are made and how much harm they have caused humanity they would not cultivate them so intensively.

104.

How do I know if I am working with the right things?

Short answer:

You have no choice.

Long answer:

How you think determines what you think. All art is a kind of self-portrait, or at least an impression of who you are, where you are, and when you are. You may not be able to determine what you are thinking about, only how much. (Just try not to think of a blue hippopotamus.) You do not control the direction, only the speed. If you want to change how you work or how you think, you should change everything around yourself instead of changing yourself.

105.
Why am I disappointed?

Short answer:

Age.

Long answer:

Most studies show that people are most disappointed around the age of 32-34 years. That is when you come to the realization that all the aspirations of your youth will not come true and you have not yet come to terms with your boring day job. Your disappointment is directly proportionate to how high your own expectations were. Later in life, when you have grown accustomed to your predicament and become more content, you can appreciate minor successes, like for instance a functional stomach, and you learn how to find joy in such matters. If you compete in big sporting events, like the Ironman Triathlon in Hawaii, with an expectation of winning, there is a big chance that you will be disappointed. Before the start, everyone has a chance to win, but in reality almost no one wins. If you participate without comparing yourself to others, you will not be disappointed – tired for sure, and probably pretty satisfied with your performance.

106.
How do I paint as similar as possible?

Short answer:

It cannot be done.

Long answer:

Many artists paint for instance "realistically" and claim that it is similar. In a picture with central perspective of e.g. a house, the windows become smaller and smaller the further away they are. Is that right? Most houses I have seen have windows of the same size along the whole length. All forms of art are a "lie" the same way that the word sandwich will never be a sandwich. In Japan they developed the parallel perspective instead, which they thought was more similar to reality, which made it hard for them understand what was portrayed in photographs in the beginning, especially all the dark patches on people's faces, since they did not work with shadows in their art.

107.

What should you learn during your schooling?

Short answer:

The ability to learn.

Long answer:

There is no point in learning things that you have no use for, such as spending a week learning how to make water-color paper if you are planning on working with video for the rest of your life, and vice versa. The types of crafts are practically innumerable and even if you master them all it says nothing about what kind of things you will make or why. I recently encountered a problem with a sick elephant and could not recall anything from my eight years in art schools that could help me in that situation. But the ability to solve problems as they arise involving different techniques and materials, is priceless.

108.

How do you know if a painting is good?

Short answer:

It depends on what you will use it for.

Long answer:

Is a dull table-knife of any use at all? Yes, if you have been locked in a freezer storage and have to unscrew a few bolts to get out, or if the knife happens to be Grandma's old table-knife that you ate with as a child (sentimental value), but it would not be of any use for cutting through leathery meat at a restaurant. Nothing is intrinsically good or bad – it depends on what you use it for. Take personal responsibility for the quality of your work and do not hide behind common norms that are changing all the time anyway.

109.

Are there any good books if you are learning to make art?

Short answer:

No, a book about tennis will work just as well.

Long answer:

There are many good books about the different crafts in art, but none about how to make good art. Books about sports, on the other hand, contain veritable gold nuggets, tips that you can apply to art. For instance: Let the ball do the job instead of rushing around the court – take advantage of the material you are working with, savor its qualities instead of forcing your own notions upon it, such that it will always resist you, and remember never to train and compete at the same time. Avoid making art all the time. Allow yourself ample time to really investigate and explore things. And looking at Björn Borg's personality, for example, it is obvious that it would have served him splendidly as an artist too.

110.

Why are you so interested in foxes?

(The most common question I get.)

Translator's note: Ernst Billgren makes a lot of foxes.

Short answer:

Which foxes?

Long answer:

When you enter a chemist's laboratory you are sure to see a lot of test tubes and you might draw the conclusion that he is interested in test tubes. I do not. He is probably interested in discovering some new enzyme or unknown element, or finding the cure to a disease. The test tubes are instruments, and he probably does not even notice them at all and lacks all interest in them, and in foxes.

111.

Does megalomania help?

Short answer:

It depends on how good you are.

Long answer:

All kinds of personalities are represented among artists, although throughout the history of art there may be an over-representation of megalomaniacs. There are different kinds of megalomania, for example: "I am the most humble of all!" and similar cases that may be difficult to discern. Choose a form of megalomania that fits your personality and your artistic career. Megalomania suits people who are already terribly good, since there is a risk that your receptiveness to information decreases and you become impervious to constructive criticism. That may tip the balance against the positive effects of the improved self-confidence that your megalomania will generate.

112.

Is it important to have good taste?

Short answer:

It is more important to be decent.

Long answer:

The better opinions people have, the worse taste they develop. For example, the styleof clothing of everything ranging from Hell's Angels to the dictators of the 20th century are often impressive and stylistically pure. I watched a program about a gang of old peacenik ladies who were going to travel around Europe in a bus and discuss peace issues. They wore white formless shifts. Who would a young disgruntled man in the 'hood' identify with?

Opinions do not determine taste – on the contrary. If those old ladies had been dressed in black uniforms with silver skulls, peace would probably have been secured a long time ago.

113.

Why is there so much written about peculiar art?

Short answer:

Purely the instinct of self-preservation.

Long answer:

If you work at a factory manufacturing red beach balls and suddenly, after ten thousand red ones have passed by, a blue ball appears on the assembly line, it will strike you as remarkable, odd and probably beautiful as well. At the store, laying side by side on the shelf, they will appear equivalent and just as good-looking and remarkable. People who write about art and spend their whole days visiting exhibitions are naturally more alert and more attentive to strange and odd specimens purely based on the instinct of self-preservation., in order not to be bored to death. In the Middle Ages there was a sparser flow of images, they were not subject to even a millionth of what we consume today, and in those days qualities other than "oddity" were prioritized.

114.

Why do people have such differing opinions about art?

Short answer:

They are speaking about different things.

Long answer:

When you compare art with art, you see that they have nothing in common with each other. When you listen to discussions about art it is like listening to a discussion between a fisherman and a shot-putter. The fisherman says: "But you cannot catch a fish that way!" and the shot-putter remarks: "You cannot throw away a shot like that!" Art is a generic term for a plethora of activities and things that have nothing whatsoever in common.

115.

How much of what you read in the newspapers about art can you trust?

Short answer:

Twenty percent.

Long answer:

An experiment was conducted where test subjects were asked to choose a picture of a person, and eventually they had to explain why they chose that picture in particular. But unknown to the test persons, when it was time to justify their choice, the picture was secretly changed. Despite this, eighty percent of the test persons proceeded to explain why they had chosen the new card, even though it was not the one they had chosen. Similarly, eighty percent of all explanations in the media about why they appreciate or detest some art can simply be ignored. They are probably actually talking about something else. One of our brain's main functions is to justify our frequently emotional decisions to us and give us a feeling that the world is intelligible and logical, and that we understand what we are doing, and why.

116.

Can you claim that if you know the most, you will be best?

Short answer:
No.

Long answer:
Most tennis trainers know much more about tennis than all the youngsters that they coach, but the trainers would not stand a chance if they were to play a match against the kids. Knowledge and skills are only interesting to the degree that they can be put into practice.

117.

What is art?

Short answer:

A way of thinking.

Long answer:

If you assume that we think through language, then art is a way of thinking about things that we lack any other language for.

Index

abroad 66	*the* bumps 55
abstract painting 37	call into question 30
advice 3, 17, 47, 74	cannonball 67
age 105	capable 89
aging artists 5	*the* center of art 43
alternative art 48	central perspective .. 106
anachronism 11	cheese 54
anti-cryptic 32	choice 40, 45, 71,
approximation 25	.... 88, 104
arrogance 79	chromatics 18
art 4, 65, 117	*a* classic 21
art school 32, 50,	colleagues 57
.... 76, 93	commenting on others' art 58
associative power 37	common norms 108
atomic bombs 68	concentration 39
atoms 4	conform 8
avoiding 91	conjecture 74
bakers 27	contemporary artist 90
beautiful (things) 33	content 44
beginner's outlook 94	conventions 16, 26,
belief systems 80	.... 34, 60
bikes 13	cookbooks 77
Björn Borg 99	create life 98
the blind spot 62	creating 40, 71
Blitzkrieg 24	criticism 32
the brain 28, 39, 115	*croquis* 18
brain surgeon 17	cross images 33
brand 38	curators 12
breakthrough 73	

Dan Wolgers 87	function 55
death 22	galleries 12, 19
defensive 91	good 2, 32, 35,
dialogue 66	.... 53, 92, 108, 109,
digital artists 89	.... 111, 112
disappointment 105	good artists 35, 91
discrepancy 6	good books 109
Egyptians 7	Goya 16
Einstein 5, 68	getting lost 36
electric shocks 61	Glenn D. Lowry 53
encouragement 56	Goodyear 31
energy 68, 98	graphic artists 89
eternity 98	green 28
exactness 25	group enterprise 57
exhibit 12, 52	Guderian 24
the Expansion of the	happy 23, 44
universe 87	hell 18
experiment 21, 74	high-strung 95
experts 17	*Home Alone* 84
failing 63, 70	ideals 23
fairness 92	idiot 94
female artists 99	idiotic opinions 88
figurative painting ... 37	ignorant 17
fire 15	impossible events 69
flaws 24	independence 16, 19,
focus 39	.... 49, 59
forget 87	indifference 6
foxes 110	infuriating people 11
frogs 19	innovation 7

intellectual 75	money 95
interviews 84, 85	musts 87
inventions 62	*the* myth 38
knowledge 1, 26, 41,	Napoleon 66
.... 92, 116	nature or nurture 97
Kokoschka 16	*the* need to
language 9, 65, 73,	express yourself 79
.... 117	non-commercial art .. 12
lazy people 47	non-conformist 46
Leftists 20	normal 33, 49
lies 74	old junk 86
life and death 68	one-man
Linnaeus .. *Introduction*	enterprises 57
listen and obey 30	opinions .... *Intro-*
luck 35	*... duction*, 6, 16, 17, 20,
magic 32	... 30, 32, 42, 59, 74, 80,
mistakes 14, 31	.... 88, 103, 112, 114
Mars 100	originality 7
masterpieces 18, 82	Orwellian lies 74
Matisse 10	painting 90
Matrix 103	painting a tree 3
meaningless 49	painting rapidly 51
the media 15	painting slowly 51
megalomania 23, 111	paradise 88
message 96	paradoxes 64
mimic 26	parallel perspective . 106
misunderstanding ... 26	peculiar art 113
Modernism 9, 73	perception 28
Mona Lisa 96	performance ability ... 14
	Picasso 10, 51, 82

Plurkevass! 73	Sex Pistols 29
the purpose of art 27	sharpen your senses 52
the point 102	shortcomings 24
politics 20	should 87
poor taste 80	*Silence of the Lambs* 83
potatoes 72	
Pre-Rafaelites 53	*the* sky 3
problems 24, 40	skylight 81
promotion 15	smug 79
provocation 11	social creatures 16
purpose 27	social realism 27
quality ..... 7, 38, 53, 55, ... 56, 82, 108	space 31
	speaking about art ... 42
quantum physics 25	specialization 29
rats 54, 61	sports 14
realistic painting 106	stagnation 5
rebellion 8, 34	stealing 101
repetition 26, 54	stealing my ideas 72
resistance 8	success 23, 50
reward system 80	taste 80, 83, 112
riding a bike 13	teachers 10, 70
the right track 36	tennis 63, 109, 116
runner-up 14	test tubes 110
satisfaction 50	Theory about Everything 5
sclerosis 29	
self-analysis 13	thinking ... 64, 104, 117
self-censure 2	toasters 1
self-confidence 8, 11	too blurred 102
self-criticism 13	

too old	56
too self-confident	64
Torsten Andersson	90
trust	16
ugly art	58, 86
unclear	25
understanding	9
Valand Art College	8
value	82, 99
van Gogh	12
Volvo	19
washing potatoes	72
ways to work	40
Weltanschauung	20
the wheel	15
The Wizard of Oz	43
Wolfgang Pauls	72
yellow triangles	100
yes-man	8
Zeitgeist	2

The What Is Series

The What Is books share a simple format, with questions posed by the authors followed by their short and long answers. The idea of the books is to provide easily absorbed knowledge about complicated subjects in a straight-forward yet entertaining manner. The What Is books are written by the foremost experts in their fields and as such the style varies between authors, though the format remains the same, providing common ground throughout the series.

What is art and 100 other very important questions (2008)
Ernst Billgren

Art is for everyone and you too can attend a vernissage and understand what people are discussing. According to Ernst Billgren, art is what makes us human. In this book, he turns the concept of art inside out and toys with its terminology. Billgren asks, "How do you know if a painting is good?", "What is taste?" and "Is it important to succeed?" Answering with wit and humour, he guides us through the book, arousing interest and curiosity far outside the world of art.

What is art II 100 new very important questions (2010)
Ernst Billgren

When you want to delve deeper into the world of art. Following the success of "What is art and 100 other very important questions", Ernst Billgren received many letters from readers wanting answers to more questions about art. He has gathered some of those questions, such as "When can I call myself an artist?", "What is quality?" and "When am I fully trained?", and you can find the answers in this book.

What is politics and 100 other very important questions (2010)
Ernst Billgren and Carl Hamilton

Dare to participate in political discussions. "How do I become a winner in politics", "How do I know what to think?", "Why do politicians behave so strangely at election time?" These questions provide the opportunity for people to formulate their own answers and to examine their true opinion. A book that offers short and long answers to your questions about politics and increases your awareness of the political arena.

What is truth and 100 other very important questions (2010)
Jonas Hallberg

Develop your philosophical side and seek out the truth with Sweden's most famous seeker. Here Jonas Hallberg poses questions such as "Are white lies necessary?", "How can your truth ever be mine?" and "Is it true that a picture is worth a thousand words?". Questions that are easy to have opinions about, but what is the real truth?

What is music and 100 other very important questions (2011)
Salem Al Fakir and Pontus De Wolfe

A guide for anyone wanting to understand different types of music. Two of Sweden's major music profiles guide you through the music landscape and pave the way for new questions about the subject you thought you already knew everything about. This book also offers useful advice on matters such as "How do you get a song out of your head?" and "How do you listen to music?" It even answers the eternal question "Who wrote the modem sound?".

What is literature and 100 other very important questions (2011)
Ulrika Kärnborg

Have you ever wondered what literature actually is and how what we call literature is created? Then this is the book for you. Ulrika Kärnborg, author and literary critic for, among others, the Swedish daily newspaper Aftonbladet, knows literature and takes you on a journey through her thoughts on the subject. Here you can pursue interesting questions such as "Why does literature tell the truth even when it lies?" and "What comes first, the reading or the writing?".

What is film and 100 other very important questions (2011)
Tomas Alfredson

If you want to learn to understand film and why it affects us so strongly. Tomas Alfredson, renowned director of films such as "Let the Right One In" and one of Sweden's most successful film exporters ever, is given a free hand to share his thoughts on film with a wider audience. He also has a chance to rant at his colleagues and to air his bitterness in this lively book.

What is sex and 100 other very important questions (2011)
Katerina Janouch

Questions most people ask themselves, but which few can truly answer. No matter how you relate to sex, sex is a subject that fascinates and provides an endless stream of interesting questions. Sweden's most well-known sex therapist deals with questions such as "Can vibrators make men unnecessary?", "Do homosexuals have better sex than heterosexuals?" and "Can you have too much sex?".

© Ernst Billgren and Bokförlaget Langenskiöld, Stockholm, Sweden
Text: Ernst Billgren. English translation: Carl Fredrik Gildea,
Eva Tofvesson Redz, Amesto Translations
Graphic design: Jan Thurell, K2AB
Composing and printing: Bulls Graphics, Halmstad, Sweden, 2011
www.langenskiolds.se
www.whatisart.se
www.questionbooks.se